# Bless the LORD!

## OBSTACLES AND OPPORTUNITIES

Yolanda "Cookie" Doyle

ISBN 979-8-88751-619-6 (paperback)
ISBN 979-8-88751-620-2 (digital)



Christian Faith Publishing
832 Park Avenue
Meadville, PA 16335
www.christianfaithpublishing.com

Printed in the United States of America

# CONTENTS

# LESSON 1

# **Bless the Lord**

*Psalm 34 is titled,* "The Happiness of Those Who Trust in God." It was written by David. Take time to read a commentary or introduction on this psalm in your Bible to discover what David experienced that inspired this poem.

Read all of Psalm 34 in one sitting. It is such a rich psalm of confidence in the Lord. It also shows us how God responds to those who fully trust him. Let's begin by examining *verse 1: "I will bless the LORD at all times; His praise shall continually be in my mouth."*

In your own words, write out what you think it means to "bless the Lord." ______________________________________________

_______________________________________________

Blessing the Lord is to recognize the goodness of God and live it out. It is to verbally communicate his goodness through prayer back to him. When we bless God, it comes out in conversations with others. It is to live, acknowledging his goodness in and toward you. To bless the Lord is not simply a mental assent but is a response seen in how we live.

*Bless* in Hebrew *(barak)* means *"to praise and to congratulate."* It is to hold in high regard the one receiving the blessing.

Read the following passages, and write out the reason or reasons God is blessed in each verse.

*Psalm 28:6* _______________________________________

_______________________________________

*Psalm 66:20* _______________________________________

_______________________________________

*Psalm 68:35* _______________________________________

_______________________________________

*Psalm 68:19* _______________________________________

_______________________________________

*1 Peter 1:3* _______________________________________

_______________________________________

*Ephesians 1:3* _______________________________________

_______________________________________

Though each of these passages is about things God has done that make him worthy to be blessed, it is because of who he is that he does what he does.

Read the following verses, and write out the characteristics of God that make him worthy to be blessed.

# BLESS THE LORD!

*Psalm 118:1* ______________________________________

___________________________________________________

*Lamentations 3:22–23* ________________________________

___________________________________________________

*1 Chronicles 29:11* __________________________________

___________________________________________________

*James 1:17* _________________________________________

___________________________________________________

*John 14:6* __________________________________________

___________________________________________________

*Matthew 7:11* _______________________________________

___________________________________________________

Our circumstances can easily take our attention away from the Lord and place it on ourselves. To choose to "bless the Lord at all times" is to be deliberate. Offering blessings to God, especially when life is difficult like it was for David, does cost us our self-perseverance and self-focus. It is to die to self.

Turn to *1 Chronicles 21:1–28*. As you read through these verses, take note of what David did and how God responded. Write down what you learn about God's character. David recognized his sinful choice and addressed God. David was commanded to build an altar.

In *verse 22*, what does David ask Ornan (Araunah) the Jebusite?

_______________________________________________

_______________________________________________

In *verse 23*, what is the price Ornan (Araunah) offers David?

_______________________________________________

_______________________________________________

In *verse 24*, how does David respond to Ornan's generosity?

_______________________________________________

_______________________________________________

Take time to meditate on David's response. *"I will surely buy it for the full price, for I will not take what is yours for the LORD, nor offer burnt offerings with that which costs me nothing."*
Many times, "to bless the Lord" costs us something. If blessing God was always easy, how would you know it was sincere?

_______________________________________________

_______________________________________________

What are you going through that you need to be purposeful in order "to bless the Lord?"

_______________________________________________

_______________________________________________

Perhaps you're struggling to see a reason to "bless the LORD." It happens. If you think the only time to "bless the LORD" is when life is good, then go back and reread some of David's life. Read from the start, when he is anointed as king, through his time running from Saul, until he is sitting on the throne as king. It was a difficult journey. David found reasons to "bless the LORD." Psalm 34 was written in the middle of some of the chaos that was David's journey. His example of choosing to "bless the LORD," I pray would help you repent of the attitude that keeps you from doing the same. "Blessing the Lord" in difficulty is to know the offering is sincere.

# LESSON 2

# Bless the Lord
## *at All Times*

As we begin this week's study, I had to laugh. We ended last week with me encouraging many of you who struggle to "bless the Lord." In this study, I'm asking you to "bless the Lord *at all times.*" I want to keep you from growling at me by saying, "Well, it is not I who asks this of you. It is our example, David, who is asking." To be more exact, it is God who demands it. We don't just find this command in *Psalm 34* but throughout the Word of God.

Let's breathe together. Bless the Lord for the opportunities he is giving us to study and know him better. Then, let's get started.

*Read Psalm 103:1–22.*

David begins by saying, *"Bless the Lord, O my soul: and all that is within me, bless His holy name."* This is a synonymous parallelism. Much of Hebrew poetry is written this way. In synonymous parallelism, a thought is repeated in different words; the second part expands the meaning or brings clarity to something said in the first part.

David says, *"O my soul; and all that is within me, bless His holy name."* How does David use synonymous parallelism to define the soul?

__________________________________________________________

__________________________________________________________

The Hebrew word for *soul* is *nephesh*, which points to appetite, desire, heart, mind, and pleasure.

Write out *Psalm 103:2* _________________________________________

__________________________________________________________

David is commanding his soul to do *"all that is within him,"* to *"forget not all His benefits." Self-talk* happens to all of us. Some of us do that out loud and humorously get accused of being a bit looney. Seriously though, we all self-talk. Sometimes we know we are doing it and other times we are unaware. Self-talk tends toward conscious thoughts that come from what we believe about any given topic. Self-talk does not have to be out of our control. David focuses his self-talk on training himself to *"forget not all His (The Lord's) benefits."*

Where have you allowed your self-talk to take you? ______________

__________________________________________________________

Do you think you are stuck with the thoughts that come to your mind? ______________________________________________

__________________________________________________________

How can you, like David, offer your soul more beneficial ways to think so that you can more easily offer blessings to God than inane or sinful thoughts? *2 Corinthians 10:5* may help. _______________

_______________________________________________

*Self-talk is a term not found in Scripture.* As believers, we are told to *"meditate day and night"* (at all times). This is actually what David is encouraging himself to do. As he commands his soul "to forget not all His benefits," what are the benefits he brings to mind? Read *verses 3–6*, and list the benefits David tells himself not to forget.

1. _______________________________________________
2. _______________________________________________
3. _______________________________________________
4. _______________________________________________
5. _______________________________________________
6. _______________________________________________

Remember in our human condition, we often think about what God does first. We look for what benefits us. David's list is similar to what we would do too. But David doesn't stop there. He knows none of those benefits would be possible if it were not for who God is.

Read *verses 8–22*, and write out a few characteristics of God that David mentions. How do the characteristics you chose to write help you bless the LORD?

1. _______________________________________________
2. _______________________________________________

3. _______________________________________________
4. _______________________________________________

When we live to see who God is and what he is doing, it becomes easier to fill most of our waking thoughts with "blessing the Lord!" I bet those thoughts would change our emotional health. Thinking of God is more beneficial than all the vacuous thoughts that fill our minds. Read *1 Thessalonians 5:16–18*, and list what we are commanded to do.

1. _______________________________________________
2. _______________________________________________
3. _______________________________________________

These adverbs should remind you of what David said about blessing the Lord in *Psalm 34:1 "at all times."* Now that you see similar commands in the New Testament, what is your responsibility?

_______________________________________________

_______________________________________________

Obedience will cost you. Yes, of course, it will. Obedience demands change. Here is the key: *God never commands what he does not empower.* God has given us his spirit. He fills us, walks with us, and offers us the strength to obey.
Read *Matthew 11:28–30*, and summarize these verses.

_______________________________________________

_______________________________________________

These verses not only communicate benefits from the Lord if we choose to yoke ourselves to him, but they also offer us the characteristics of his peace. To "bless the LORD at all times" should not be a burden. God wants to help us think or meditate about him. Our soul is encouraged by this activity.

Read *Hebrews 12:1–2*. What things are we directed to do?

_______________________________________________________

_______________________________________________________


What characteristics of Jesus does the author point out?

_______________________________________________________

_______________________________________________________


The author also offered us an example from Jesus's outlook. What is that example? ___________________________________________

_______________________________________________________


How much should we desire to be like Jesus by choosing to follow David and "bless the LORD at all times?" _______________________

_______________________________________________________


What keeps you from emulating David? _______________________

_______________________________________________________


How would a change in "self-talk" from self-absorbed conversation to commanding your soul to "forget not his benefits" change your outlook on life? _________________________________________

_______________________________________________________

Do a study on the characteristics of God. Pick out two or three, and find scripture that exemplifies these characteristics. Write them out. Has there been a time in your life where one of these characteristics of God has been seen? Take time to list God's benefits in that situation, and then end your time of study by "blessing the LORD."

Characteristic one _________________ Benefit _________________

Characteristic two _________________ Benefit _________________

Characteristic three _______________ Benefit _________________

Use these lines to finish if needed. _______________________

_______________________________________________________

In the following lessons, we are going to walk through the lives of biblical characters who let circumstances dissuade their choice to "bless the LORD." They allowed emotional obstacles and negative self-talk to put their focus on themselves. Though we all do it, it does not make it acceptable.

Those examples will be Elijah, Naomi, and Jonah. First, Elijah's life will show us the *obstacle of self-pity*. Next, we will look at Naomi, the mother-in-law of Ruth. She will teach us how to overcome the *obstacle of bitterness*. We will also look into the life of Jonah. He will take us through the *obstacle of pride*. Though eventually, Jonah did what God wanted, he would not do it with an obedient heart. He even shows us he knows God's character. Yet he did not relent from his sinful anger. As we finish his story, we will read that he would not "bless the LORD." We will look carefully at the things God does in each of these lives that reveal his person, his care, and his benefits. We will see God's encouragement and rebukes for lacking the kind of faith that sees his benefits no matter what we are facing.

After looking at each of these examples, we will observe Psalm 34 and see how David chose to see through the opposite lenses in his circumstance. Instead of *self-pity*, he looked through the lens of *joy*; *hope* for *bitterness* and *humility* instead of *pride*. Each of us has these choices before us. As we study these lives, we get to step back, look at our circumstances, and decide what we will believe about God. Then we decide how we will walk through our circumstances.

We are told in *Hebrews 11:6, "But without faith, it is impossible to please God because any who comes to him must believe that he exists and that he rewards those who earnestly seek him."*

Wait! "*He rewards* those who earnestly seek him?" Another benefit that offers reasons we can "bless the LORD at all times." "He rewards." What has kept you from seeing God's benefits in whatever circumstances you are facing? ________________________________

________________________________

Briefly share a testimony of running the race faithfully that has been set before you? ________________________________

________________________________

What does it look like in life to choose joy, hope, and humility daily?

________________________________

________________________________

End this week's study by making a list of benefits from God that you can bless him for. *Then take some time to "bless the LORD."*

In the next few weeks, we will study what kept Elijah, Naomi, and Jonah from "blessing the LORD at all times." Their stories will teach us so much. The Scripture is for our benefit (*Romans 15:4*). See what I pointed out there? "For our *benefit?*"

# LESSON 3

# The Obstacle of *Self-Pity* (Elijah's Story)

Read *1 Kings 17. Then list each of the characteristics and benefits God showed Elijah in each of the sections listed below.*

*Verses 1–7* _______________________________________

_______________________________________

An interesting tidbit of Bible knowledge: God feeds Elijah with a raven, yet a raven is among the "detestable" birds named by God in *Leviticus 11:13* and repeated in *Deuteronomy 14:14. Detestable* doesn't mean hate. God cares for the ravens (*Job 38:40–41; Psalm 147:9*). In *Luke 12:24*, Jesus reminds the disciples that God feeds the ravens. There is so much to bless the LORD for in this tidbit.

*Verses 8–16* _______________________________________

_______________________________________

In the following verses, Elijah encounters his first hiccup. Up to now, things are going smoothly. There is no reason for him not "to bless the LORD." He calls for a drought. God provides food and drink.

When the brook dries up, God already has Elijah's provision ready. Though times are tough, the path is smooth. Then comes the test: the son of the widow dies. Read Elijah's words carefully. What do you pick up when you read verse 20?

*Verses 17–24* ___________________________________________

_______________________________________________________


Reread *verse 1*, and take note of the confidence. Then read *verse 20*. Do you sense a difference? _________________ If yes, write your thoughts out. _______________________________________

_______________________________________________________


There already seems to be a tinge of self-pity in his words, *"O LORD my God, have You also brought tragedy on the widow with whom I lodge, by killing her son?"* What an accusation of God's character! The great thing here is that Elijah moves on through his feelings and prays in faith, *"Let this child's soul come back to him."* God hears Elijah, and just like with the drought, he acts in the affirmative through Elijah's faith.

*"Elijah was a man with a nature like ours, and he prayed earnestly that it would not rain; and it did not rain on the land for three years and six months" (James 5:17).* Get out your favorite commentaries or Bible footnotes, and study what it means to say *"a man with a nature like ours."* _______________________________________

_______________________________________________________


Read *1 Kings 18:20–40*. Before we summarize these verses and the characteristics and benefits shown to Elijah and also to Ahab and the people of Israel, let's write out *verse 22 (NKJV): "Then Elijah said to the people,* ______________________________________________ *but Baal's prophets are four hundred and fifty men."* The part you wrote out actually feeds into Elijah's self-pity.

Read *verses 2–14.* What did Obadiah, not the author of the Bible book with that name, tell Elijah? ______________________________

______________________________________________

Turn to *1 Kings 19:1–4.* Summarize these verses.

______________________________________________

______________________________________________

What was Elijah's prayer? ______________________________

______________________________________________

Remember in Psalm 34, David was running for his life, but the words that came from David's heart then came out of his mouth, *"I will bless the LORD, at all times. His praise shall continually be in my mouth."* How does David's mindset while facing the possibility of death differ from Elijah's thinking as he faces the possibility of death, *Psalm 43:5?*

______________________________________________

______________________________________________

We see a bit of a theme with Elijah when he faces obstacles. First, with the death of the widow's son. Second, being alone did not mean he was the only one. God brought Elijah and Obadiah into contact with one another to encourage Elijah. There was a benefit for Elijah to take in and hold to the character of God. Sadly, he communicated not from the reality of God's faithfulness in his life and the lives of many prophets. Instead, Elijah communicates from, I don't know, perhaps *emotions, exhaustion, or exaggeration.* For all of this, an obstacle moves in Elijah's way: the obstacle of self-pity.

*Read 1 Kings 19:10,14,* and summarize how Elijah repined to God.

_________________________________________________

_________________________________________________

*Read verse 18.* Write out how God corrected Elijah?

_________________________________________________

_________________________________________________

Elijah had information about the character of God that could have allowed him to "bless the LORD." Self-pity may easily be fomented by exhaustion, loneliness, hunger, and other physical maladies. This could happen while you are busy with God's work. Self-pity doesn't have to be related to sin in your life. Elijah was doing God's work, and yet we can see self-pity. *Self-pity is an unhealthy, obsessive sorrow for oneself arising from a selfish viewpoint of one's circumstances.* If you go back and read David's life, you will see opportunities for him to wrestle with self-pity. We don't read that about him. There are stories in the life of David that parallel, not exactly, but to a spiritual degree, with those of Elijah.

*What does David say in Psalm 34:1?* Write it out. _________________

_________________________________________________

Read *1 Samuel 30:1–6.* Summarize *verse 6* _____________________

_________________________________________________

Read *Psalm 43:5*. David recognized the sadness in his soul, possibly self-pity. "Why are you cast down, O my soul? *And why are you disquieted within me?* [Fill in the next part] ________________________

___________________________________________;

*For I shall yet praise Him, the help of my countenance and my God."*

*Self-pity* may come when you least expect it. The feeling is not a sin. The warning, though, is that if the feeling comes, it must be dealt with instantly and aggressively. We cannot make room for self-pity. It will thwart our ability to see the character of God. It will blind us to the benefits of God in any given circumstance we are living through. While we celebrate the faith of Elijah, we would be remiss not to study the struggle he faced with a *"nature like ours."*

How have you faced off with self-pity to keep it from stopping you in a pursuit to "bless the LORD?" _______________________

______________________________________________

Maybe you don't recognize self-pity. Perhaps God is identifying it in you as you have gone through this lesson. If you identify it now, what might you do so you can begin "to bless the LORD" and assuage the feeling of self-pity? ______________________________

______________________________________________

God will not magically take away your circumstances. He wants to build your faith through them. You must choose *"to bless the LORD!"*

## The Happiness of Those Who Trust in God

I will bless the Lord at all times; His praise
*shall* continually *be* in my mouth.
My soul shall make its boast in the Lord;
The humble shall hear *of it* and be glad.
Oh, magnify the Lord with me,
And let us exalt His name together.
I sought the Lord, and He heard me,
And delivered me from all my fears.
They looked to Him and were radiant,
And their faces were not ashamed.
This poor man cried out, and the Lord heard *him,*
And saved him out of all his troubles.
The angel of the Lord encamps all around those who fear Him,
And delivers them.
Oh, taste and see that the Lord *is* good;
Blessed *is* the man *who* trusts in Him!
Oh, fear the Lord, you His saints!
*There is* no want to those who fear Him.
The young lions lack and suffer hunger;
But those who seek the Lord shall not lack any good *thing.*
Come, you children, listen to me;
I will teach you the fear of the Lord.
Who *is* the man *who* desires life,
And loves *many* days, that he may see good?

Keep your tongue from evil,
And your lips from speaking deceit.
Depart from evil and do good;
Seek peace and pursue it.

The eyes of the Lord *are* on the righteous,
And His ears *are open* to their cry.
The face of the Lord *is* against those who do evil,
To cut off the remembrance of them from the earth.
*The righteous* cry out, and the Lord hears,
And delivers them out of all their troubles.
The Lord *is* near to those who have a broken heart,
And saves such as have a contrite spirit.
Many *are* the afflictions of the righteous,
But the Lord delivers him out of them all.
He guards all his bones;
Not one of them is broken.
Evil shall slay the wicked,
And those who hate the righteous shall be condemned.
The Lord redeems the soul of His servants,
And none of those who trust in Him shall be
condemned. (Psalm 34:1–22 NKJV)

# LESSON 4

# An Opportunity for *Joy* (Psalm 34:1–7)

Read *Psalm 34:1–7*. Summarize things about David from *verses 2–7*.

_______________________________________________

_______________________________________________


Summarize what David says about God. _______________________

_______________________________________________


*Psalm 34* is attributed to David when he was feigning madness before Abimelech. Abimelech is the title of the king of Philistia. Abimelech is not a personal name. I wanted to bring clarity to that because we are going to read the story. Depending on your Bible translation, you may run into the title Abimelech or possibly the name Achish. The latter is the personal name of the king. Both are speaking of the same person.

Turn to *1 Samuel 21:10–15*. Let's observe why the words from the servants would have caused David concern. Read *1 Samuel 18:5–9*. What was said in both passages? ________________________________

________________________________________________________

In *chapter 18*, how did those words from the women affect the relationship between David and Saul? ____________________________

________________________________________________________

Turning back to *1 Samuel 21:10–15*, what was David's reaction to Achish the king of Gath's servants repeating this reprise? __________

________________________________________________________

How might this have been a reasonable reaction? ______________

________________________________________________________

With all that in mind, read *Psalm 34:1–7* again. David is choosing to "bless the LORD." He is inviting others to "magnify the LORD with me." Read *1 Samuel 22:2*. List how the passage describes those who were with David. _______________________________________

________________________________________________________

David becomes the leader of these troubled men. As David's struggles become theirs, it would be easy for David to lead them into self-pity and more distress. Instead, David offers them an invitation. Write out *Psalm 34:3*. ___________________________________________

________________________________________________________

David knows that not everyone can "magnify the LORD" with him. In the second part of verse 2, who is it that he says will hear this invitation? _______________________________________

______________________________________________


David is not talking about physically hearing, but his words are similar to Jesus's in *Matthew 11:15: "He who has ears, let him hear."* David recognizes those who have spiritual ears are humble. We will address that characteristic after we talk about the obstacle of pride through the lesson of Jonah.

Let's pause and work through what the Bible teaches us about *joy*. Through biblical research, *joy* is said to be a condition of our souls that we are given by God's spirit (*Galatians 5:22*). In this passage, Jesus lets his disciples know that their *joy* will be full if they keep his commands and remain in his love (*John 15:10–11*). Experiencing biblical *joy* is a choice in the middle of hard circumstances. It is chosen by those who understand that hard circumstances produce patience and are part of God completing and perfecting our lives (*James 1:2–4, 12*). Read each of the above passages, and write a definition of *joy*. _______________________________________

______________________________________________


Joy doesn't need to be absent of feelings; however, we cannot count on feelings to assure the experience of joy. Think through all you have read about David's circumstances in *1 Samuel 21*. From what David says in *Psalm 34:1–7*, what hints are offered that he was experiencing the joy of the LORD? _______________________________

______________________________________________

In *1 Samuel 21:12,* what emotion does David experience?

_______________________________________________

_______________________________________________

This emotion militated his actions. How did David act, *verse 13,* when he thought he might be in danger? ____________________

_______________________________________________

One of my favorite things about the Bible is that we are not left to believe our heroes, like David, were perfect. For a moment, David's flesh led his behavior. He acted in fear. But unlike Elijah, who needed to be coaxed by God because he was experiencing self-pity, David did not take long to recognize his fear and cry out to the LORD. Write out *Psalm 34:4.* ____________________________________

_______________________________________________

While we don't see in *1 Samuel 21* that David cries out to the LORD, Psalm 34 tells us what he did in his fear. Not only does David let us know in his psalm that he cries out to the LORD, but he also tells us that his men are looking to him without shame in *verse 5.* What might have caused them to be ashamed? ____________________

_______________________________________________

What does *Psalm 25:3* tell us? ___________________________

_______________________________________________

Write out Psalm 34:6. _____________________________________

_______________________________________________

When David says, *"The LORD heard him, and saved him out of all his troubles,"* in context, he was saved when he feigned madness that got him cast out of Abimelech's presence. We've already addressed the fear that motivated David to put on this act. I previously purported that this act was an error of judgment, perhaps a lack of faith. That is a conclusion that I read in a few commentaries. I don't necessarily agree. Let's consider his reaction as him seeing that "the LORD… saved him out of all his troubles." You may not agree with what you are going to read, but allow me to propose something.

There is a natural adrenaline response God has given to the human race. When we face life-threatening situations, we respond with *fight, flight, and freeze.* To *fight* is to put yourself in a position to face any given situation hands-on. *Flight* looks for a way out of danger. Perhaps not telling the truth makes a path to escape. For example, you are being robbed and the attacker asks, "Do you have a weapon?" Looking for an opportunity to flee and having a gun strapped around your waist, you respond, "NO!" Your response isn't so you can hurt someone. While hoping to escape, you know you may still have an opportunity to protect yourself if he doesn't check you. Is your response a lack of faith? Is it an inherent natural reaction to self-preservation endowed to us by God? Perhaps you quietly prayed to God for a way out, and this was what came to mind. I am not going to belabor the point. You can completely disagree with my premise. I am not developing doctrine or have one in mind that I'm pulling from. Let's continue with *freeze.* It is exactly that, being unable to move against any given threat.

Back to *Psalm34:6*, who does David credit for "saving him out of all his troubles?" _______________________________________________

_______________________________________________________________

You'd think he could have given his quick thinking credit, but he didn't. How does he describe his disposition?___________________

_______________________________________________________________

Look up the word *poor man* in a Bible dictionary.

_______________________________________________________________

_______________________________________________________________

Does the definition of him as a "poor" man give insight into David's perspective of his life at that time? ___________________________

_______________________________________________________________

David's life-threatening experience offered him the opportunity to see life through the *Lord's joy*. How does what we have studied so far from *Psalm 34* help you understand how being *"afflicted"* or *"poor"* in David's eyes isn't self-pity? _____________________________________

_______________________________________________________________

Are there any thoughts that come to mind as you have allowed me to offer you what I think about David's feigning madness? Please present your argument. ___________________________________________

_______________________________________________________________

Read *Psalm 34:7*. We will get some background on David and where he might have received such confidence in the LORD. What does *Psalm 34:7* tell us about "the angel of the LORD?" _______________________

_______________________________________________________

"The angel of the LORD" is what theologians call a *theophany* (an appearance of God) in the Old Testament.

We need to go back to the Bible's introduction of David in *1 Samuel 16*. Read the entire chapter, and jot down some bullet points.

_______________________________________________________

_______________________________________________________

After David was anointed, what did the spirit of the LORD do?

_______________________________________________________

_______________________________________________________

How did God gift David to be used in *two* ways to aid Saul physically and spiritually? _____________________________________

_______________________________________________________

Read *1 Samuel 17*. Summarize the chapter. _________________

_______________________________________________________

In *verse 26*, how does David define Goliath? _______________

_______________________________________________________

What does he call the Israel army? _________________________

_______________________________________________________

In *verses 31-37*, what does David propose to Saul?

____________________________________________________

____________________________________________________

What were the two experiences David shares to show he was ready for battle? _________________________________________

____________________________________________________

Though it was David who had to face the threat, in whom did he place his confidence in *verse 37*? ________________________

____________________________________________________

In *verses 45–47*, as David faced off with Goliath, what was his shout before he even had a victory? __________________________

____________________________________________________

Finish the passage from *verse 47*. David did not want his own glory, but the victory would be that *"all this assembly may know*

____________________________________________________

_________________________________________________."

Turn back to *Psalm 34:7*. Put into words how all you just previewed from David's early life brings him again to the conclusion of what he wrote in *verse 7*. _________________________________

____________________________________________________

Let's end by comparing how David could have as easily encountered self-pity but instead chose the joy of the LORD while facing life-threatening difficulties. We see from what we studied that there were men who looked to his example and were not ashamed of their choice to follow David. His example was that of faith and joy as his strength from the LORD.

How can you, like David, choose faith and joy so that you "bless the LORD"? _________________________________________________

_________________________________________________

Remember, the choice to follow David's example is not to pretend your obstacles don't exist. The choice "to bless the LORD" by walking in joy and then inviting others to "magnify the LORD" with you is to believe he is doing a work for your good and his glory. How does your life show you believe that? _______________________________

_________________________________________________

Take time to tell your soul not to forget God's benefits this week. What are some of those benefits? ___________________________

_________________________________________________

# LESSON 5

# The Obstacle of *Bitterness* (Naomi's Story)

*Loss* is such a horrible part of life. Only a psychopath can lose someone and not be affected. Jesus wept at the death of Lazarus, whom he loved, even though he knew he was going to raise him from the dead. Loss makes life more difficult. We will all face it. Many of us have faced it already. Whether we are losing someone we are familiar with or someone we love deeply, both are life-impacting and perhaps life-altering. Loss and grieving are exemplified in the Bible so we can learn how God wants to help us through it. We will look at the life of *Naomi*, the mother-in-law of Ruth, as an example. Loss, for her, was life-altering. The loss also became associated with *bitterness*. Let's study how her life helps us see how to avoid the bitterness that will always prevent us from being able to "bless the LORD."

Open your Bible to the book of Ruth. Read *chapter 1:1–5*, and answer the following questions. What is the name of the man we are introduced to in verse 2? ______________________________

______________________________________________________

What was his wife's name? _______________________________________

_______________________________________________________________

Where were they from? _________________________________________

_______________________________________________________________

Where were they living and why? ________________________________

_______________________________________________________________

What happened to Elimelech? ___________________________________

_______________________________________________________________

Look up the meaning of the name *Naomi.* _________________________

_______________________________________________________________

From reading the first five verses, we learn that life was not truly "pleasant" for Naomi due to the circumstances her family was in before the death of Elimelech, Naomi's husband. Before he died, in a foreign land, she had her husband to care for her.
Who else was with Elimelech and Naomi? __________________________

_______________________________________________________________

We read that the two sons were married. Where were their wives from? ___________________________________________________________

_______________________________________________________________

What are the names of the wives? ________________________________

_______________________________________________________________

How long had this family lived in Moab? ________________________

_________________________________________________________


Sadly, Naomi's life would become less "pleasant" than her name claims. What happened to her sons? ________________________

_________________________________________________________


Let's look at the relationship between the Moabites and Israel. Read *Judges 10:6*. The Moabites were a stumbling block to Israel in this passage. We see Israel serving the gods of the Moabites. We are not going to do a full study of Israel and the Moabites. I wanted us to have a background to Naomi's storyline. We now know she was in the land of Israel's enemies. Her sons married Moabite women. What was God's law concerning intermarriage with idolatrous nations? Read *Deuteronomy 7:1–6* and summarize what God says about these marriages. _______________________________________

_________________________________________________________


Read *Numbers 25:1–5*. What had Israel's men done that garnered God's anger? _______________________________________

_________________________________________________________


When we read the Bible, we find a variety of literary types. As we read the book of Ruth, since the book takes place during the period of the Judges, we are reading history. History does not always pause to correct God's people who were living the antithesis of his law. There is a difference between literature in the Bible that describes facts. These facts, when we do not read of God's intervention where sin is present, can lead us to believe God permits or, worse yet, accepts the choices of the people who we are reading about. Remember, facts are in view, information not an endorsement of behavior. Facts are not teaching us theology outright. There is also that, which we call prescription. A prescription outlines God's commands. Prescription, that which God lays out to be obeyed, helps us read a narrative and see where the character is in or out of line with God's law when reading descriptive history.

When we read the information about Naomi and Elimelech, we are looking into a description of their lives. As we review, like we just did, we can make some conclusions about how their lives line up with how God prescribed for his people to live. While we must always be careful not to make conclusions that are not clear in the Bible, we can put information together that allows for safe orthodoxy.

When in a place where our lives are already in error with God's word, as life hits us, we may find our view of God in error. This will cost us emotionally and physically. A bad understanding of God or living in deliberate disobedience will never go without impacting our lives. Read *Ruth 1:1–5*, and write out where their lives are not in line with God's prescription from what we have previously reviewed.

———————————————————————————————

———————————————————————————————


First, Naomi became a widow. Then her daughters-in-law became widows too. All three of these women were out of the care of a husband. In this case, there was also no son to care for any of them. We must remember that being a widow then is not at all like being a widow in our time. Women were completely dependent on their husbands, their sons, or those whom God's law put in place for their care. The Israelite community was commanded to care for widows, orphans, and the poor. This care would not govern the country of Moab, where Naomi was living. Let's look at what God set up in his law for the protection and care of these aforementioned groups, which Naomi found herself.

Read the following passages, and summarize what they say.

*Deuteronomy 24:17* _______________________________________

_______________________________________________________

*Psalm 68:5* ____________________________________________

_______________________________________________________

*Isaiah 1:17* ___________________________________________

_______________________________________________________

Israel was given special instructions on how to care for widows, orphans, and the poor. These laws were familiar to God's people. They were obligated to live by these laws to be God's holy people. Read *Ruth 1:6–7.* What decision did Naomi make?

_______________________________________________________

_______________________________________________________

Why did she make this choice? ____________________________

_______________________________________________________

In some translations, verse 6 says, *"The Lord had visited His people by giving them bread."* Another translation for *visited* is *attended to.*

Write out from verse 1 why Naomi's family was in Moab.

_____________________________________________

_____________________________________________

In verse 6, what did God provide for the people of Israel?

_____________________________________________

_____________________________________________

We know there was a famine. We know Naomi's family was in Moab for ten years. During the time period they were in Moab, God began providing bread for Israel. Let's speculate a little. Perhaps the family did not need to go to Moab. Instead of looking to God, Elimelech trusted his own ability to provide and moved to a place where God forbids intermarriage for his people. Yet intermarriage happened. Yes, I've belabored this point because it is urgent for us to understand. We must walk in obedience to the LORD in order to see the benefits of his guidance and care, especially during the difficulties of life. When life becomes chaotic and circumstances turn us upside down, being able "to bless the LORD" is difficult if we don't truly know who he is, what he commands, and what he promises. Let's get back to Naomi and when she begins to declare God as her problem.

Naomi suggested her daughters-in-law go back to their families. What were her blessings to them, *1:8–9*? _____________________

_____________________________________________

Naomi sent them with the wish of God's blessing on them. For God to "deal kindly" is in Hebrew the word *hessed*, which is a "mercy given by a more powerful being over a weaker." Do some research on this word. Write out some of your discoveries.

___________________________________________________

___________________________________________________

Read *verses 11–13*. How does Naomi see her situation?

___________________________________________________

___________________________________________________

We cannot always say our bad circumstances are God's discipline. Read Job after you've done this study to grasp a handle on that reality. Naomi declares her circumstances as coming from the "hand of the LORD." What are some of the conclusions you can come up with to say she may be correct? _________________________________

___________________________________________________

As we continue to read, we will observe that one of her daughter-in-law's, Orpah, chose to go back to her family, while the other, Ruth, chose to go with Naomi. Let's skip a couple of verses. Write out *verse 20.* _______________________________________

___________________________________________________

What does this verse display about the character of Naomi to you?

___________________________________________________

___________________________________________________

How do you think she can pray for God's blessings on her daughters-in-law and yet change her name to Mara, which means *"bitter?"*

_______________________________________________

_______________________________________________

Do you believe her view of God has changed?

_______________________________________________

_______________________________________________

Are there things in your life that make you believe *"the Almighty has dealt very bitterly"* with you? ___________________________

_______________________________________________

Have you sought God in this situation? ___________________

_______________________________________________

I won't dare say your situation is due to sin in your life, but I will ask, is your life in line with God's commands and teachings?

_______________________________________________

_______________________________________________

It is possible your situation is simply life. It is possible your situation is a purposefully crafted sanctification God is taking you through. There is also the possibility that what Naomi was about to do is your need as well. She was headed back to where God wanted her to be over the last ten years: to Judah, where his presence is. For you and me, perhaps we need to repent and return to the right relationship with him. Take time to examine your thoughts, life, your heart, your attitudes, and then your actions. Is your life more associated with "Moab?" This is to be in a place God does not want you to be. Are you in need of returning? Write out a prayer of confession or one that tells your soul "to bless the LORD" and then we will get back to "Mara" next week.

# LESSON 6

# *Outwitting Bitterness*
# (God's Weapons in the Battle)

Read *Ruth 1:1–20* again to begin our week. Write out verse 20.

_______________________________________________

_______________________________________________

There are two views of *verse 20.* Some believe Naomi was expressing the facts of her circumstances. She was not accusing God but expressing her circumstances that happened because her family was not in obedience to God. What do you think of this commentary?

_______________________________________________

_______________________________________________

Others believe she was making a complaint against God. They see this due to what she says next. Summarize *verse 21.* _______________

_______________________________________________

What do you think of the latter commentary? _______________

_______________________________________________

Which is your conclusion as to why Naomi is now seeing herself as "bitter"? ___________________________________________

_____________________________________________________

Let's look into how God helps us outwit bitterness in his power. The *Merriam-Webster* dictionary defines *bitterness* as 1.) sharpness of taste; lack of sweetness. 2.) anger and disappointment at being treated unfairly; resentment. The *Merriam-Webster* dictionary defines *outwit* as 1.) to get the better of by superior ingenuity or cleverness; outsmart. to outwit a dangerous opponent. 2.) surpass in wisdom. Whichever of the two commentaries on Naomi seeing herself now as Mara, "bitterness," or a different conclusion, we can agree she does not see her life filled with the pleasantness of God, Yahweh. In Naomi's circumstances, no matter where they originated, she understood what she must do to experience the sweetness of Yahweh again. *Outwitting bitterness starts with:*

1. *Returning to God*—Read *Ruth 1:7, 16–19, 22.* Naomi did not disabuse Ruth of desiring the God of Judah to be her own God. Do you think Naomi still knew the God of Judah to be the only true God?

_____________________________________________________

_____________________________________________________

Bitterness can paralyze us. This strong emotion can foment apathy and lethargy if we do not recognize it right away and return to God. Read the following verses and summarize them.

*1 John 1:9* ___________________________________________

_____________________________________________________

*Luke 6:46* _______________________________________________

_______________________________________________

*Hebrews 9:28* ___________________________________________

_______________________________________________

How do these help you see the benefits of returning to God and leaving bitterness behind you? ________________________________

_______________________________________________

2. <u>*Remembering you are not your own*</u>—Write out *1 Corinthians 6:19.*

_______________________________________________

_______________________________________________

Summarize *Philippians 3:12–13* ________________________________

_______________________________________________

If we have claimed Jesus as LORD, we cannot, at the same time, claim ownership of ourselves or anything God has given us to manage. When we come to Jesus, we exchange allegiance from one kingdom to another. We have a new king. Read *2 Corinthians 4:6; Colossians 1:13; 1 Thessalonians 2:11–12;* and jot down some conclusions.

_______________________________________________

_______________________________________________

How do you think understanding our lives from God's perspective as not belonging to us helps us to outwit bitterness? ________________

_______________________________________________

Read *Ruth 1:1–7.* How does Naomi recognize God's care for his own?

______________________________________________

______________________________________________

When we understand that in Christ, we belong to God, we begin to hold loosely to this world and the things in our life. That is not to stop caring, but to know God tells us this is not our home. We are also told this world is moaning and impacted by sin and death. We are impacted by sin and death in this world, and nothing that impacts us is because God wants to destroy us. In my Psalm 73 study, we go through the reasons why we go through hardships (trials). You can do that study or do your own research. If we keep our eyes on our hardship, we will become bitter. Hebrews 12:2 tells us, *"Let us fix our eyes on Jesus."* If you and I are owned by God, like a child focusing on their dad and mom, we hold eye contact with our LORD during circumstances that can invite bitterness into our lives.

Let's look at what Naomi did. She knew God was covering Judah at times of need and famine. She remembered that she knew God's provision and needed to get back to him. That is the next way God has set up for us to outwit bitterness.

3. *Recognize God's covering*—Read *Matthew 14:22–31.* Summarize Peter's part of the story. ______________________________

______________________________________________

How did Jesus view his fear? ______________________________

______________________________________________

Fear and doubt are considered "little faith" to Jesus in this scenario.

What do the following cross-references say about bitterness?

*Acts 8:23* ______________________________________________

____________________________________________________________

*Colossians 3:8* __________________________________________

____________________________________________________________

*Ecclesiastes 7:9* ________________________________________

____________________________________________________________

*Ephesians 4:26* __________________________________________

____________________________________________________________

*James 1:19–20* __________________________________________

____________________________________________________________

*Hebrews 12:14–15* _______________________________________

____________________________________________________________

What does this last passage in Hebrews tells us can happen with bitterness? ________________________________________

____________________________________________________________

God has given his children coverings so "that no bitter root grows up to cause trouble and defile many."

*A. Walking in the Spirit (Romans 8:1–11)*
What has God done for us in his Son (*verses 2–4, 10–11*)?

______________________________________________

______________________________________________

What are the contrasting ways of living offered to us?

______________________________________________

______________________________________________

Why does the choice we make on how we live cover us from bitterness taking root (*verses 6–8, 9–10*)? ______________________

______________________________________________

*B. Wearing his armor (Ephesians 6:10–18)*
Write out *verse 10.* ______________________________

______________________________________________

What is the goal of the armor from that verse? ______________

______________________________________________

No matter what you are going through, how does *verse 12* put it in perspective? ______________________________________

______________________________________________

While the Scripture is replete with passages that show and tell us that people are responsible for their choices to bring harm into others' lives, God wants justice and righteousness from people. Sadly, more often than not, we suffer at the hands of other humans. How does God in Ephesians 6 want us to view this kind of suffering?

_______________________________________________

_______________________________________________

In *verse 13*, what does the armor of God give us the ability to do?

_______________________________________________

_______________________________________________

*Verse 18* brings us to prayer. It keeps us watchful. It helps us persevere through troubling times. Read *James 1:12*. What is the character of the person who perseveres? _______________________________

_______________________________________________

Perseverance proves we love him according to this verse. What is the reward for the one who perseveres? _______________________________

_______________________________________________

How is Naomi showing perseverance through bitterness? Read *Ruth 1:6–7, 16–19, 22.* _______________________________________

_______________________________________________

*C. Waiting in prayer (Philippians 4:6–7)*
This passage admonishes by saying, *"Be anxious for nothing."* How is that possible? _______________________________________

_______________________________________________

Write out the rest of *verse 6*, "but ___________________________

_______________________________________________________

It appeared that Naomi understood what God had done and that she needed to be back where God was working. Her story tells us that she recognized the "bitterness" of life that had impacted her. She wanted to go home. The place of God's presence.

In this Philippians passage, *"the peace of God"* is offered. What does God's peace do according to this passage?_____________________

_______________________________________________________

How does prayer outwit bitterness? _______________________

_______________________________________________________

Look up some commentaries on *"the peace of God…will guard your hearts and minds through Christ Jesus."* Write out some important points you'd want to share. _________________________

_______________________________________________________

*Bitterness is dangerous!* We cannot keep it from coming up as part of life's difficulties. There are no passages where God says, "I will take bitterness from you." Like Naomi had to make some decisions to get back to where God's presence was, we too must make decisions to obey all the warnings and remedies to bitterness.

*In God's presence is fullness of Joy (Psalm 16:11).* Naomi knew this. His joy is a remedy for bitterness. That is found in God's presence. Naomi headed home. We don't have to travel to put ourselves in the presence of God to experience his joy. We may need to begin with repentance.

*God will keep us in perfect peace, "whose mind is stayed" on Him, Isaiah 26:3–4.* Naomi knew this. Her bitterness would only be turned to peace after getting out of the compromised position she was in. Moab was an enemy country. God forbade his people to intermarry with them. Naomi made this right and again, headed home. Receiving this perfect peace is conditioned on our minds staying on him.

Go back through some of the passages from this week's study on *outwitting bitterness*. List the conditions God puts on us to be victorious over the venomous emotion of bitterness.

______________________________________________

______________________________________________


Where does all of this leave you if you are facing bitterness?

______________________________________________

______________________________________________

# LESSON 7

# The Opportunity for *Hope*
# (Psalm 34:8–14)

Read *Psalm 34:1–14.*

Turn to *1 Samuel 21:10–15,* and refresh your memory on what David was facing that brought about *Psalm 34.*

David had been anointed by Samuel to become God's chosen king. He was adored by the people of Israel as a mighty warrior for defeating the Philistine military champion, Goliath. The Israelite maidens attributed tens of thousands of defeated foes to David. And now David was on the run for his life from King Saul. In 1 Samuel 21, he'd run from these warriors for fear of being seen as a threat. Those who followed him were a motley group living in caves. What reason would David have to become bitter? _______________

_______________________________________

What does he say to those with him in *Psalm 34:8?*

_______________________________________

_______________________________________

How does this declaration reveal David's heart "to bless the Lord?"

_______________________________________________

_______________________________________________

He not only expresses the benefits for which he blesses God but also understands God's desire to bless us back. Whom does God bless?

_______________________________________________

_______________________________________________

Remember, Naomi and her family went to Moab due to a famine in Israel. Maybe out of a lack of faith, or perhaps carelessness on Elimelech's part to consider what God said, he looks to his own ability to provide.
What is the hope found in David (*Psalm 34:9–10*)?

_______________________________________________

_______________________________________________

David found provision in God's temple. Read *1 Samuel 21:3–6*. What is David given to eat and feed his men?

_______________________________________________

_______________________________________________

There is so much in this story. The opinions are all over the place about the sinfulness, or lack thereof of David, eating the showbread and not being a priest *(Lev. 24:5–9)*.
Read *Matthew 12:1–7; Mark 2:18–28; Luke 6:1-5*. What was happening in this story? _____________________________

_______________________________________________

David was in violation of the letter of the law. What was Jesus's explanation for David and his disciples? _______________________

___________________________________________________

What is Jesus's desire in *Matthew 12:7*? _______________________

___________________________________________________

Whether Jesus was speaking more to the inconsistencies of the Pharisees or teaching a greater lesson about the law, we can debate. David, as the anointed king of Israel, was never confronted for this act. God sent Nathan to confront him and call him to repentance for his acts of adultery and murder. God cannot overlook moral sin because it would go against his character. He does not seem to see it as an affront to his character that David took, broke, and shared the showbread with his hungry men. Perhaps this goes back to "description" versus "prescription." I'll let you come to your own conclusions. What perspective does David have about the situation in *Psalm 34:10*? _______________________

___________________________________________________

What perspective does Jesus offer in *Matthew 7:9–11*? _______________________

___________________________________________________

David knows he and his men are in a precarious situation. He chose to focus on God's care for them and not the turbulence of his life. We covered this. Here is an opportunity for meditation. How is David's handling of his circumstances, if adopted by you, a way to biblically outwit bitterness and view things with hope? _______________________

_______________________________________________________________

David took time to see his circumstances as an opportunity for hope, "to bless the LORD" by speaking life to those with him. How did he see these men in *Psalm 34:11*? _______________________

_______________________________________________________________

David expressed practical choices we must make to experience hope over bitterness. David realized that "to bless the LORD" means we must deal with our words and our actions. Bitterness is easily heard in what we say, then seen in what we do. We get to choose both. Our words and actions lead to death or life. They matter the most when life is challenging us or has brought us deep pain. We are not excused in these circumstances to sin. David outlined to his men how they should be speaking. Perhaps they just finished eating the showbread. Perhaps they were hungry again, and he reminded them of God's provision. Perhaps bitterness was beginning to rise in some of them. David's encouragement in *verses 12–14* leads to hope and outwits bitterness. What does David encourage in verses 13–14?

1. _______________________________________________

2. _______________________________________________

3. _______________________________________________

4. _______________________________________________

5. _______________________________________________

6. _______________________________________________

These requirements are for those described in *verse 12*? Write out how they are described. _______________________________________

_______________________________________

The Bible promises many things. One of those things is trouble or tribulation. Summarize John *16:33*. _______________________

_______________________________________

We are hidden in Jesus, who has overcome the world. He offers us this hope so we can find the benefits of his victory in whatever we are facing. Those situations will be used by our common enemy, the devil, to destroy us, but God allows them for our good. Jesus gives us his peace.

My goal is not to make you ashamed if you are experiencing bitterness. Hope is available. Summarize *Proverbs 28:13*.

_______________________________________

_______________________________________

Talk to someone, then like David poured out life into those with him, find others who need your testimony. They need you to tell them how they can find the opportunity for hope so they may be able to "bless the LORD."

Imagine how Naomi's story could have ended if she chose not to return to God, where bitterness is destroyed. Perhaps there would not have been a Ruth in Jesus's lineage. Jesus would have had another ancestor, but maybe her name would have been something else.

Imagine David's story if he chose bitterness over hope. Yes, that's a lot to imagine. Thank God we do not need to imagine that. We can read his story of not holding on to bitterness over Saul. In fact, let's read *2 Samuel 1*. Saul's death put David in his rightful position, but he did not celebrate. He mourned. Read *verses 17–27, and* write out the ways David describes Saul and Jonathan. _______________________

_______________________________________________________________

When we read Psalm 34, we can have confidence in the sincerity with which David speaks of his hope in God. We know that his "blessing the LORD, at all times" is true. No one who hides bitterness can say the things he said about a man who considered him a threat and tried frequently to kill him.

It is imperative that we face our bitterness and, if possible, those by whose hands it fomented. What does *Ephesians 4:26* command of us?

_______________________________________________________________

_______________________________________________________________

Anger that is unresolved will turn to bitterness. I wonder if David's circumstances were running through his head while on the run. Instead of capitulating to something he could not change and the feelings that come with it, he chose to encourage his men about hope (Psalm 34:11–14). We have choices. We can give in to the feelings that accompany every hard circumstance. We can remember all that God's spirit offers us and the tools he offers to outwit bitterness.

David ends by saying, *"Seek peace and pursue it."* How can seeking peace and pursuing it in whatever hardship you are facing release you from the feeling of bitterness and give you the opportunity for hope and help you "to bless the LORD?" _______________________

_______________________________________________________________

Now the word of the Lord came to Jonah the son of Amittai, saying, "Arise, go to Nineveh, that great city, and cry out against it; for their wickedness has come up before Me." But Jonah arose to flee to Tarshish from the presence of the Lord. He went down to Joppa, and found a ship going to Tarshish; so he paid the fare, and went down into it, to go with them to Tarshish from the presence of the Lord. But the Lord sent out a great wind on the sea, and there was a mighty tempest on the sea, so that the ship was about to be broken up. Then the mariners were afraid; and every man cried out to his god, and threw the cargo that *was* in the ship into the sea, to lighten the load. But Jonah had gone down into the lowest parts of the ship, had lain down, and was fast asleep. So the captain came to him, and said to him, "What do you mean, sleeper? Arise, call on your God; perhaps your God will consider us, so that we may not perish." And they said to one another, "Come, let us cast lots, that we may know for whose cause this trouble *has come* upon us." So they cast lots, and the lot fell on Jonah. Then they said to him, "Please tell us! For whose cause *is* this trouble upon us? What is your occupation? And where do you come from? What is your country? And of what people are you?" So he said to them, "I *am* a Hebrew; and I fear the

Lord, the God of heaven, who made the sea and the dry *land.*" Then the men were exceedingly afraid, and said to him, "Why have you done this?" For the men knew that he fled from the presence of the Lord, because he had told them. Then they said to him, "What shall we do to you that the sea may be calm for us?"—for the sea was growing more tempestuous. And he said to them, "Pick me up and throw me into the sea; then the sea will become calm for you. For I know that this great tempest *is* because of me." Nevertheless the men rowed hard to return to land, but they could not, for the sea continued to grow more tempestuous against them. Therefore they cried out to the Lord and said, "We pray, O Lord, please do not let us perish for this man's life, and do not charge us with innocent blood; for You, O Lord, have done as it pleased You." So they picked up Jonah and threw him into the sea, and the sea ceased from its raging. Then the men feared the Lord exceedingly, and offered a sacrifice to the Lord and took vows. Now the Lord had prepared a great fish to swallow Jonah. And Jonah was in the belly of the fish three days and three nights. (Jonah 1:1–17 NKJV)

## Jonah's Prayer and Deliverance

Then Jonah prayed to the Lord his God from the belly of the fish, saying, "I called out to the Lord, out of my distress, and he answered me; out of the belly of Sheol I cried, and you heard my voice. For you cast me into the deep, into the heart of the seas, and the flood surrounded me; all your waves and your billows passed over me. Then I said, 'I am driven away from your sight; yet I shall again look upon your holy temple.' The waters closed in over me to take my life; the deep surrounded me; weeds were wrapped about my head at the roots of the mountains. I went down to the land whose bars closed upon me forever; yet you brought up my life from the pit, O Lord my God. When my life was fainting away, I remembered the Lord, and my prayer came to you, into your holy temple. Those who pay regard to vain idols forsake their hope of steadfast love. But I with the voice of thanksgiving will sacrifice to you; what I have vowed I will pay. Salvation belongs to the Lord!" And the Lord spoke to the fish, and it vomited Jonah out upon the dry land. Then the word of the Lord came to Jonah the second time, saying, "Arise, go to Nineveh, that great city, and call out against it the message that I tell you." So Jonah arose and went to Nineveh, according to the word of the Lord. Now Nineveh was an exceedingly great city, three days' journey in breadth. Jonah began to go into the city, going a day's journey. And he called out, "Yet forty days, and Nineveh shall be overthrown!" And the people of Nineveh believed in God. They called for a fast and put on sackcloth, from the greatest of them to the least of them. The word reached the king of Nineveh, and he arose from his throne, removed his robe, covered himself with sackcloth, and sat in ashes. And he issued a proclamation and published through Nineveh, "By the decree of the king and his nobles: Let neither man nor beast, herd nor flock, taste anything. Let them not feed or drink water, but let man and beast be covered with sackcloth, and let them call out mightily to God. Let everyone turn from his evil way and from the violence that is in his hands. Who knows? God may turn and relent and turn from his fierce anger, so that we may not perish." When God saw what they did, how they turned from their evil way, God relented of the disaster that he had said he would do to them, and he did not do it. But it displeased Jonah exceedingly, and he was angry. And he prayed to the Lord and said, "O Lord, is not this what I said when I was yet in my country? That is why I made haste to flee to Tarshish; for I knew that you are a gracious God and merciful, slow to anger and abounding in steadfast love, and relenting from disaster. Therefore now, O Lord, please take my life from me, for it is better for me to die than to live." And the Lord said, "Do you do well to be angry?" Jonah went out of the city and sat to the east of the city and made a booth for himself there. He sat under it in the shade, till he should see what would become of the city. Now the Lord God appointed a plant and made it come up over Jonah, that it might be a shade over his head, to save him from his discomfort. So Jonah was exceedingly glad because of the plant. But when dawn came up the next day, God appointed a worm that attacked the plant, so that it withered. When the sun rose, God appointed a scorching east wind, and the sun beat down on the head of Jonah so that he was faint. And he asked that he might die and said, "It is better for me to die than to live." But God said to Jonah, "Do you do well to be angry for the plant?" And he said, "Yes, I do well to be angry, angry enough to die." And the Lord said, "You pity the plant, for which you did not labor, nor did you make it grow, which came into being in a night and perished in a night. And should not I pity Nineveh, that great city, in which there are more than 120,000 persons who do not know their right hand from their left, and also much cattle?" (Jonah 2:1–10; 3:10; 4:1–11)

# LESSON 8

# **The Obstacle of *Pride* (Jonah's Story)**

Read *Jonah chapter one* (copy included). I love how this chapter begins. God is offering an opportunity for trust. He knows what we presume about what will be Jonah's response, yet God still calls on Jonah to act obediently. The story begins with the word *now.* That word offers us a time reference. On whose behalf was God moving in *verse 2?* _______________________________________________

_______________________________________________

At this point in this study, I want you to do some research on Nineveh. On a separate sheet, take some notes on your research. In *verse 2*, Nineveh is called *"that great city."* We also learn that it is a great city being called out *"for their evil."* What does your research bring to light?

Before we get into the text, let's do a short study on the sovereignty of God. We hear that characteristic of God frequently. How would you define the sovereignty of God? _______________________________

_______________________________________________

Look up the word *sovereignty* in the dictionary. Write out its meaning(s). ___________________________________________

______________________________________________

Many times, when we hear someone using the term "God is Sovereign," they sometimes mean *omnipotent*. The difference between the two is that the sovereign is the ruler or leader; omnipotence is the power exhibited. A sovereign exhibits the power to rule. As we go through the text of Jonah, we will see God's sovereignty. We will also see his omnipotence. His omnipotence will help us see what kind of sovereign he is. Are you confused yet? In order to understand what kind of ruler God (Sovereign) is, we must examine his actions. In Jonah, we will see that. The first word, *now*, begins that examination.

How does the word *now* in this text help you understand God as a Sovereign? ___________________________________________

______________________________________________

Let's review a few verses that exhibit both the sovereignty and omnipotence of God. Read the passage, and write out the two distinctions below. In each verse, what words describe his sovereignty? Which words describes his omnipotence?

*Sovereignty Omnipotence*

Colossians 1:16 ___________________________________

______________________________________________

Psalm 115:3 _______________________________________

______________________________________________

Isaiah 40:28 ______________________________________

______________________________________

Nehemiah 9:6 ______________________________________

______________________________________

Psalm 50:11 ______________________________________

______________________________________

It may be that you only see one or the other attribute. They work hand in hand. However, in order to understand sovereignty, we must look at how God exercises his power and right to rule. How would you sum up these characteristics, their similarities, and their differences? ______________________________________

______________________________________

The entire book of Jonah displays these two characteristics of God. As we look at the obstacle of pride in Jonah, I believe they will stand out all the more. Especially now that I've brought them to the forefront. Just as a reminder, the word *now* offers us a time reference. As the sovereign, God chose the timing to step into "the great evil" of "that great city," Nineveh. How does God choose to act?

______________________________________

______________________________________

What was Jonah's response? ______________________________________

______________________________________

This response teaches us a lot about God's way of ruling as well. What does it teach you? _______________________________

_______________________________

Write out the first five words of verse 3. _______________________________

_______________________________

Write out the first eight words of verse 4. _______________________________

_______________________________

We will learn so much more about why Jonah responded to God's command the way he did in chapter 3. Here we see the chutzpah of Jonah to outright disobey God in this way. The timing of this call to Jonah was at the peak of Nineveh's power. It was prior to Assyria's invasion of Israel.

There is truly an arrogance that allows for such a despising of God's command. I am sure you can relate. Think of someone you may despise. They may have caused you great pain, and God calls you to share your faith with them. Perhaps he puts on your heart, *Go to such and such. Let them know they will die in fourteen days. Tell them I say, "Repent and turn to God."* Would this be a struggle for you?

_______________________________

_______________________________

Would you immediately act in obedience? _______________________________

_______________________________

Would you consider God's ability and right to discipline you?

_______________________________________________

_______________________________________________

Why would you not care about the soul of that individual when God does? _______________________________________________

_______________________________________________

We are called to "bless the LORD" at all times. How does this scenario get in the way of that? _______________________________________________

_______________________________________________

How does Jonah's disobedience show the obstacle of pride?

_______________________________________________

_______________________________________________

Read Jonah 1:4–6. Who is impacted by his hard-heartedness?

_______________________________________________

_______________________________________________

In *verse 5,* what were the mariners' reactions to the turbulent seas?

_______________________________________________

_______________________________________________

What was Jonah's reaction to the turbulent seas?

_______________________________________________

_______________________________________________

What was God calling Jonah to do? ___________________________
_______________________________________________________

What was Jonah's first reaction? ____________________________
_______________________________________________________

What was Jonah's second reaction? __________________________
_______________________________________________________

What was Jonah's third reaction on the ship? ________________
_______________________________________________________

Write out *Proverbs 8:13.* ___________________________________
_______________________________________________________

How does Jonah's dismissal of God's call show a lack of "the fear of the LORD?" _________________________________________
_______________________________________________________

Read Jonah *1:7–16.* We read that the men cast lots to "know on whose account this evil has come upon" them. Obviously, the lot fell on Jonah. They inquired about Jonah. Write out Jonah's answer in *verse 9.* ___________________________________________________
_______________________________________________________

In *verse 10,* what did the men find out, and who told them?
_______________________________________________________
_______________________________________________________

In verse 9, Jonah acknowledges the sovereignty and omnipotence of God. Can you point out the two? *Sovereignty*: ___________________

_______________________________________________________________

*Omnipotence*: ___________________________________________

_______________________________________________________________

I do not know about you, but these short verses take me through a range of emotions. I rejoice that God responded to the sin of an evil nation by offering them an opportunity for repentance. My heart repines over Jonah's actions. Let's imagine when Jonah was first confronted by God's plan, he chose to "bless the Lord" in what he heard and was asked to do. I've heard people say, "But look at the way Jonah's encounter with the mariners turned out for them."
Write out *verse 16*. ________________________________

_______________________________________________________________

When God uses our disobedience and pride to bring an outcome that blesses him, it is never a reason to rejoice or excuse our disobedience and pride. There are *never* any rewards for *sin*! Seeing God's sovereignty in this part of Jonah's story shows us his goodness, that he can use our disobedience for his purposes. We still suffer.
Why do you think I'm using pride to describe Jonah?

_______________________________________________________________

_______________________________________________________________

*Pride—a high or inordinate opinion of one's own dignity, importance, merit, or superiority, whether as cherished in the mind or as displayed in bearing, conduct, etc.*

We can already see how there was no "fear of the LORD" in the heart of Jonah. But what do his actions show about his heart for the people God wanted to offer forgiveness to? _______________________

_______________________

Jonah instructed the mariners in *verse 12*. Write out what he says.

"_______________________

_______________; then the sea _______________

_______________, for I know _______________

_______________ is because of me."

When we read that verse, we can conclude that Jonah wanted to die. This would be the first time, but it won't be the last. Read chapter 4, verses 5–8. Write out verse 8. _______________________

_______________________

Why was Jonah so desperate to die in this verse? _______________________

_______________________

From all we've read about Jonah, who was his *only* concern?

_______________________

_______________________

How would this attitude be attributed to an inability to "bless the LORD? _______________________

_______________________

Read *Jonah 1:17; 2:1–10.* Instead of repenting, Jonah is met by the omnipotence of God. How does God display his power in *verse 17?*

_______________________________________________

_______________________________________________

An inflated view of oneself can show up in suicidal thoughts. We saw that with Elijah. We now see this with Jonah. It is pride that is motivating Jonah's depression. God does not relent to our pity. He will not capitulate to our bitterness. God does not depart from his will because we have sinful views of ourselves. He will continue to work in a way that refocuses us. The ways he uses are not always things to bring us happiness. Look at where Jonah is now.

Read *chapter two.* You will see hints of humility. *List below* the verses that stand out to you from Jonah's prayer.

_______________________________________________

_______________________________________________

Write out *verse 10.* It is another manifestation of the sovereignty and omnipotence of God. ______________________________________

_______________________________________________

Jonah is back on dry land. Compare chapters *1:1–2* with *3:1–2.* Where are we in 3:1–2? ____________________________________

_______________________________________________

What is the spiraling impact on lives between verses 1:1–2 and 3:1–2? ________________________________________________

_______________________________________________

Write out Proverbs 16:18. __________________________________

__________________________________________________________

Write out James 4:6. ______________________________________

__________________________________________________________


When God commanded Jonah to do something he knew Jonah would struggle with, God stood ready to give Jonah grace to obey, even to obey joyfully. As James says, "God resists the proud; he gives grace to the humble." We will read that Jonah will finally do what God commands him to do. We will observe that obedience is not filled with joy but is resentfully done. Even though he does what God wants, he still is not finding it in himself to "bless the LORD."
When was the last time you did what you knew was the right thing to do in obedience to God and felt nothing but resentment?

__________________________________________________________

__________________________________________________________


If you think back on that time, what about it made you resentful?

__________________________________________________________

__________________________________________________________


Briefly summarize chapter 3.________________________________

__________________________________________________________


God is also *omniscient*. He sees not only now but also tomorrow. I do believe the reason *now (1:1)* was the time for God to send a message to Nineveh was because he saw that the people would repent. One hundred years after this story, in the book of Nahum, their destruction would be predicted. Sin would run rampant again. The people would not remember nor repent.

Look up and write the meaning of *aggrandize*.

_______________________________________________

_______________________________________________

Self-aggrandizing would be my summation of 4:1–3. Jonah would consider no one but himself. In light of the good work God did, Jonah chose resentment. In his pride, he saw only what he wanted. God did so much more for others. Write out verse 2. "Ah, Lord,

_______________________________________________

_____________________________________________."

Take those words. Think about what Jonah is saying. He had the information that would allow him to obey and "to bless the Lord." Instead, from chapters 1 to 4:3, he chose himself.

At this moment, what thoughts come to mind?

_______________________________________________

_______________________________________________

Is there any situation God is bringing up where repentance is necessary? Maybe you are recognizing how pride or self-aggrandizing is causing God to resist you. Perhaps God wants to show you that any depression you may be facing is not a mental health issue but a pride issue, an issue of him fighting against you. He is calling you to repentance and back to a place where you will bless him. Take time to pray about that. Unless the answer is already clear.

Read *Jonah 4*. Focus on verses *3, 8, and 9b*. What are Jonah's wishes for himself? ___________________________________

___________________________________

Is this coming from mental health or sin? ___________________

___________________________________

What are the circumstances surrounding his desire to die?

___________________________________

___________________________________

Let's finish with Jonah. Read *4:10–11*. How do we see Jonah's pride in these two verses? ___________________________

___________________________________

What was at stake if God gave up on Jonah and simply destroyed Nineveh? ___________________________

___________________________________

What do you think was Jonah's priority? ___________________

___________________________________

Even to the end of this story, we read Jonah resentfully luxuriating in himself. God had to remind him of others. God has the last word in this story. We don't know if Jonah ever stops "to bless the LORD." It appears from all we've read that pride thwarted his ability to see the good work of God with gratitude. Jonah missed the privilege of being used by God in this amazing grace story due to his attitude.

Let's finish by looking at a couple of New Testament passages that we can meditate on to remember how God calls us to behave toward our enemies. Summarize the following passages:

*Matthew 5:44* ________________________________________

________________________________________

*Matthew 22:36–39* ________________________________________

________________________________________

Jonah knew these truths about God. He called God *gracious, merciful, slow to anger, and full of love.* That was also something he resented about God. Those characteristics of God are imposed on those who call Jesus Lord. We are called to offer *grace (Ephesians 4:29; Colossians 4:6, and 1 Peter 4:10).* Summarize those passages.

________________________________________

________________________________________

We are called to grant mercy (*Matthew 5:7*). Summarize this verse.

________________________________________

________________________________________

In *James 1:19*, what are we told to be slow to do?________________

________________________________________

What does *verse 20* say about man's or human's anger?

________________________________________

________________________________________

Application for the obstacle of pride from Jonah's story is to understand God's grace toward us before he asks us to offer it to others. God should easily expect his children to willingly "bless the LORD at all times." We aren't asked to offer him blessings from a place where we haven't lived his blessings toward us first.

# The Opportunity
# for *Humility*
# (Psalm 34:15–22)

As I write this study, I am wrestling with the reality of wanting vengeance against someone who hurt one of my children. As I finished writing Jonah, the obstacle of pride, this experience would be weeks later. I returned back and forth to the computer to complete this study and found my thoughts circuitous and my fingers limp and nothing connecting in order to sit and finish. After a very real near-death experience happened to my oldest daughter at the hands of someone she loved, I could easily connect to Jonah's frustration of ministering to someone he only wanted to hate. I remembered some verses from the book of Jonah:

> *When God saw what they did, how they turned from their evil way, God relented of the disaster that he had said he would do to them, and he did not do it. (Jonah 3:10)*

*"But it displeased Jonah exceedingly, and he was angry. And he prayed to the Lord and said, "O Lord, is not this what I said when I was yet in my country? That is why I made haste to flee to Tarshish; for I knew that you are a gracious God and merciful, slow to anger and abounding in steadfast love, and relenting from disaster."* (Jonah 4:1–2)

As I examined how I was feeling, I remembered what Jesus has done, not just for me but for all of his enemies: *"But God demonstrates His own love towards us, in that while we were still sinners, Christ died for us"* (*Romans 5:8*). How then could I not obey the command found in *Matthew 5:44? "But I say to you, love your enemies, bless those who curse you, do good to those who hate you, and pray for those who spitefully use you and persecute you."* I realized God's command does not abdicate the need for justice because this person acted in a way that could have taken a life. He needed to be held legally accountable to keep him from possibly harming another woman. While I know that was happening, I would struggle horribly if God told me to meet with the person in jail and minister to him. "Tarshish" looked a lot better to me than a trip to "Nineveh."

Read *Psalm 34*. Let's focus on the last part of this beautiful and revealing psalm. After I wrestled my emotions into obedience with the LORD, *Psalm 34:15–22* brought me from the obstacle of pride to the place where I saw the opportunity to "bless the LORD" humbly. Even in the chaos of my circumstances or whatever you are facing, what is the promise of verses *15–16?* Write them out.

_________________________________________________

_________________________________________________

While *verse 16* tells us, *"The Lord is against those who do evil,"* humility does not wait for our enemies to face that but for them to come to the Lord in surrender. In *verses 15–22*, David willingly did what Jonah didn't want to do for his enemies: David offered them clarity on two futures, one for the righteous and the other for the wicked. God warns because he loves.

Read and summarize *2 Peter 3:9.* ________________________________

__________________________________________________________________

We know God will separate these two groups on the last day. Read *Matthew 25:31–46* and summarize. ________________________________

__________________________________________________________________

Who is your "Nineveh" person that God wants you to see as he does? __________________________ They may have hurt you deeply or perhaps hurt someone you love. You may not be sent to them, but perhaps in your heart, if God asked you, you wouldn't go. Your wish for them may be for them to get what they deserve. What does *Romans 3:23* say, and why is that important to the humble?

__________________________________________________________________

__________________________________________________________________

David recognized God's care through deep pain, threats, and hate toward him. His life was threatened soon after being anointed king. After years on the run from enemies, he recognized something about God through all of it. What does he say in Psalm 34:*17–18*?

__________________________________________________________________

__________________________________________________________________

Who does God save from verse 18? ___________________________

_____________________________________________________

Look up *contrite* and write out the meaning. ___________________

_____________________________________________________

The word *contrite* in Hebrew is transliterated as *daka*, meaning *crushed, oppressed, humbled.* David chose to look to God instead of those who wished him harm, remembering the impetus of this psalm. He recognized what God promised him, and therefore, David rested in the anointing of God, which would put him in his rightful place as king.

While God saved David physically, is God saving us from physical harm or death a necessity in order to be true to his character seen in this verse? _______________________________________

_____________________________________________________

In the next few verses, we see a pause from David sharing his own circumstances, running from Abimelech, and we see a messianic shadow. Verse 20 looks forward to Jesus on the cross, and in *John 19:36* we read, *"These things happened so that the scripture would be fulfilled: 'Not one of his bones will be broken.'"* We will not deal with that, but I'd be remiss not to make mention of this verse. What is the promise of verse 19? __________________________

_____________________________________________________

Let's look at a few cross-references to identify how God *delivers him out of them all*" (afflictions). Read the following passages. Write out what you learn when facing afflictions.

Matthew 26:36–56_______________________________________

_______________________________________


2 Corinthians 12:6–10 ___________________________________

_______________________________________


John 16:32–33 ___________________________________________

_______________________________________


Hebrews 11:32–40 ________________________________________

_______________________________________


Hebrews 12:1–17 _________________________________________

_______________________________________


We obviously learn from these cross-references that God allows us to suffer and die for him. His delivery may be through death.

If you agree, how does this harmonize with the words of David, "But the LORD delivers him out of them all," with the truths of what we see in the cross-references? _______________________________

_______________________________________


At the start of this lesson, I shared that I was right smack dab in the middle of a wicked action that affected one of my daughters. It's easy to read *Psalm 34:21–22* and become puffed up.

Read verses 21–22 and write down the keywords. Next to the keywords, write out what thoughts come to mind, using 1–4 words.

*Keyword Thoughts*

___________________ - ___________________

___________________ - ___________________

___________________ - ___________________

___________________ - ___________________

___________________ - ___________________

Look up and write out the definition for *humble.*

_________________________________________

_________________________________________

*Biblical meaning for humility*—freedom from pride or arrogance.
*The humble*—recognize their needs while not embracing a falsely modest attitude. False modesty is when a person pretends to have a low opinion of his or her own abilities or achievements (*Cambridge English Dictionary*).
Did your definition connect with the biblical meaning or address false modesty? How? _____________________________

_________________________________________

*Read John 3:22–36.* What was the conflict in these verses? ________

_________________________________________

Write out *John 3:30–31.* _________________________

_________________________________________

What would it mean for you to adopt John's attitude of humility?

_______________________________________________

_______________________________________________

*Psalm 34:21–22* can be read from two vantage points. What would be the focus if you read these two verses with pride?

_______________________________________________

_______________________________________________

Write out *James 2:13.* _______________________________

_______________________________________________

These verses are a true outcome that is repeated in the New Testament. Judgment of the wicked is taught over and over in the Bible. Sadly, Jonah wanted the condemnation of an entire people. That is pride. We have no right to think of ourselves as more worthy of redemption while others deserve condemnation.

What would be the focus if you read *Psalm 34:21–22* with humility?

_______________________________________________

_______________________________________________

Write out *Matthew 5:7.*_______________________________

_______________________________________________

How do we take advantage of the opportunity "to bless the LORD" in humility when it comes to those who live a life of wickedness?

_______________________________________________

_______________________________________________

Write out *Micah 6:8.* ______________________________

______________________________

How does the Micah verse sum up *Psalm 34:15–22?*

______________________________

______________________________

Let's end this week by reviewing Jonah and then *Psalm 34.* God's mercy is extended toward his enemies. We saw that in the book of Jonah. Jonah's pride got in the way of acting in God's mercy toward an enemy. He was not able to "bless the LORD" at this opportunity. Yet God forced his hand. The entire capital of Assyria, Nineveh, repented. Jonah never changed his attitude. He was actually disappointed at the salvation of an entire people. David understood the mercy and justice of God. We should desire God to show mercy to others because we experience it daily.

Write out *Lamentations 3:22–23.* ______________________

______________________________

When does God show mercy? ______________________

______________________________

Yet when we read *Psalm 34:21–22,* we read that there is a time when God must bring justice. He does eventually to Nineveh (Assyria). Write out a summary of the book of *Nahum.*

______________________________

______________________________

How do the two books, Jonah and Nahum, go together?

_______________________________________________

_______________________________________________

God desires that none would perish, yet he holds everyone accountable. He offers opportunities for salvation. How does that help you walk humbly with your God and toward others?

_______________________________________________

_______________________________________________

How does humility help you "to bless the LORD" in relation to those you could easily have a Jonah attitude toward?

_______________________________________________

_______________________________________________

God reveals a key truth about justice to David in these last verses of Psalm 34. He experienced God's deliverance from his enemy. He understood the reality of manifold troubles; he'd faced them. He was remembering them as he wrote this Psalm. God offered this insight to the righteous and wicked to David. This was not so David could become bellicose, full of himself, and puffed up with pride. Knowing the heart of God and his love for mankind helped David to live humbly before God. Pride causes us to turn our backs on those we think don't deserve the same mercy God shows us. Humility sees others as God does and warns them of the words in _Psalm 34:15–22_.
Read _Psalm 34:15–22_. Write out a prayer with these verses in mind.

_______________________________________________

_______________________________________________

Look at the heart of Jonah one more time. This is looking in the face of pride:

> *When God saw what they did, how they turned from their evil way, God relented of the disaster that he had said he would do to them, and he did not do it.* (Jonah 3:10)

> But it displeased Jonah exceedingly, and he was angry. And he prayed to the Lord and said, *"O Lord, is not this what I said when I was yet in my country?* That is why I made haste to flee to Tarshish; *for I knew that you are a gracious God and merciful, slow to anger and abounding in steadfast love, and relenting from disaster."* (Jonah 4:1–2)

While David recognized truths about God, so did Jonah. What were those truths? _______________________________________

_______________________________________

Sum up all that you've learned in a couple of sentences.

_______________________________________

_______________________________________

How do you show humility in a conflict?

_______________________________________

_______________________________________

How will your understanding of God, from the passages we've studied this week, keep you in a place of humility?

_______________________________________________

_______________________________________________

It is *impossible* to "bless the LORD" from pride. Our enemies must be given to the LORD for him to deal with, while you pray for them and their salvation. When you can do the latter, you can rejoice, bless the LORD, and know that a heart of humility is developing in his beloved child, you.

# LESSON 10

# Your
# Obstacles
# or
# Opportunities

Write out from memory what it means "to bless the Lord." ________

_______________________________________________

"Blessing the Lord" is to recognize the goodness of God and live it out. It is to verbally communicate his goodness through prayer back to him. When we bless God, it comes out in conversations with others. It is to live, acknowledging his goodness in and toward you. To truly bless God is not simply a mental assent, but it is necessary to respond by how you and I live.

*Bless* in the Hebrew (*barak*) means *to praise and to congratulate.* It is to hold in high regard the one receiving the blessing.

Read *Psalm 34.* What are 2–3 verses that really impacted you and why? Use a separate sheet if necessary. _______________________

_______________________________________________

Why is it important to identify obstacles that will keep you from blessing the LORD? _________________________________________

_________________________________________

Which of the three obstacles dealt with in this study would be the most familiar to you? _______________________________

_________________________________________

What is your story with this obstacle? _____________________

_________________________________________

What was the opportunity that challenged the obstacle? How did it help you? ____________________________________________

_________________________________________

Now there is an opportunity for you to do some of your own studies. I want you to think of an obstacle you may face that is different from the ones studied. If you use one of the previously studied obstacles, use a different biblical story as an example. Name it and connect it to a Bible study character and how they exhibited this obstacle.

*I.*
Name the obstacle. _____________________________________

_________________________________________

What biblical character helps you understand this obstacle? _______

_________________________________________

Where is the story found in the Bible? ________________________

________________________________________________________

Summarize the story with any conclusions. Use a separate sheet if necessary. ____________________________________________

________________________________________________________

________________________________________________________

________________________________________________________

*II.*

Now do research on a biblical character who found an opportunity to "bless the LORD."

Name the opportunity ____________________________________

________________________________________________________

What biblical character helps you understand this opportunity? ____

________________________________________________________

Where is the story found in the Bible? __________________________

________________________________________________________

Summarize the story with any conclusions. Use a separate sheet if necessary. ____________________________________________

________________________________________________________

________________________________________________________

________________________________________________________

It takes a lot to admit if you are still struggling with obstacles. The only concern is hiding whatever that may be. When we bring things to light, we step into Jesus's abundance. We keep the enemy from robbing, stealing, or killing us spiritually. Write out *John 10:10*. ____

______________________________________

You make the choice to be robbed or to live in the abundance that Jesus gives. If you are wrestling with an obstacle, find a safe, wise, grace-filled, and truthful follower of Jesus to confess your sin to. "To Bless the Lord" at all times is not an option but a command. What will it take for you to obey? _______________________________

______________________________________

*Before we end, I want to thank you for faithfully digging into this topic with me.*

In my thirty-four years of walking with the Lord, I had to learn these truths the hard way. I wish there was someone who taught me that I get to choose obedience; it doesn't just happen. Also my emotions did not need to dominate my life in any adverse circumstance. The choice to obey brings God's grace and allows for a successful Christian walk. One where I can "bless the Lord at all times."

Jesus sent his spirit to walk with us and to live in us. A successful Christian walk is not one absent of difficulty, personality challenges, or stumbling. It means identifying the obstacles, the sin, and repenting, then acknowledging what "thus says the Lord," and then doing it!

While this study brings light to areas God despises and warns us against in Scripture—self-pity, bitterness, and pride—we are not left without knowing what we are commanded to put on or to choose in lieu of (*Ephesians 4:22–24*). *Self-pity is buried in joy; bitterness is destroyed with hope; and pride is resisted through humility.* There is nothing you struggle with that God's Word is not the remedy for. The Word may not address some specifics that we may think of in this 2022-era, with its fancy new ideologies. There is still the truth found in the Bible that will directly or indirectly set you free from *every* lie. *"His divine power has given us everything we need for a godly life through our knowledge of him who called us by his own glory and goodness" (2 Peter 1:3 NIV).*

My prayer for each of you is that you learn to put the brakes on the emotional rollercoaster that creates upheaval in your life. You get to make this choice. That does not mean you will not experience them, but you will not be controlled by them. You will be set free by Jesus and discover the victory you get to walk in as a Christ-follower.

I remember one of my daughters coming to me and sharing a nightmare she had. The idea of going to bed that night loomed over her, making for a dreadful day. I sat her down and told her, "Do you know you can talk to your dream self and remind yourself you are dreaming. Your dream or nightmare may still be scary, but if you take control of it, there's less chance of the fear overtaking you. While you are sleeping, say to your dream self, 'Hey, this is a dream. This is not real. Wake up!'" She used that and woke up the next morning and was overjoyed that her fearful experience in a dream did not overwhelm her.

How do these two relate? You and I no longer need to allow our circumstances to drive us to an emotional state that controls our lives. We get to identify the truth of God and trust him for it during any life obstacle. My daughter did not always wake up right away from her bad dreams, but she knew she'd wake up faster than she did before she learned she was not the victim of her nightmares. As believers, we must grab this truth. We are not victims of our circumstances or need to get exhausted by ministry. We don't have to be tossed to and fro by life. Once we understand that, we will handle things patiently, trusting that God will step in and *wake us up* spiritually.

Wake you up to what? Read and meditate on the following passage of scripture. It is a passage that woke me up to what God's Word offers in every area of life. Now I say to my soul, "Bless the Lord, at all times" and "Don't forget his benefits."

It's been my joy to serve you through this study.

> *The law of the Lord is perfect, converting the soul;*
> *The testimony of the Lord is sure, making wise the*
> *simple;*
> *The statutes of the Lord are right, rejoicing the heart;*
> *The commandment of the Lord is pure, enlighten-*
> *ing the eyes;*
> *The fear of the Lord is clean, enduring forever;*
> *The judgments of the Lord are true and righteous*
> *altogether.*
> *More to be desired are they than gold,*
> *Yea, than much fine gold;*
> *Sweeter also than honey and the [f]honeycomb.*
> *Moreover by them Your servant is warned,*
> *And in keeping them there is great reward.*
> *Who can understand his errors?*

*Cleanse me from secret faults.*
*Keep back Your servant also from presumptuous sins;*
*Let them not have dominion over me.*
*Then I shall be blameless,*
*And I shall be innocent of great transgression.*
*Let the words of my mouth and the meditation of*
*    my heart*
*Be acceptable in Your sight,*
*O Lord, my strength and my Redeemer. (Psalm*
*    19:7–14)*

# ABOUT THE AUTHOR

Yolanda "Cookie" Doyle has been married for thirty-five years to her husband, Marlon. They live in Brookshire, Texas. They have five adult children and seven grandchildren. Before moving to Texas in 2018, they lived in Spanaway, Washington, for thirty years. God developed her gifts and love for writing and teaching the Bible over those years.

She began a ministry called Renewed Women and helped many develop a biblical worldview through everyday life and challenges. She has been a mentor and counselor for over twenty-five years. She has been a speaker at various retreats. Her passion is helping Christian women grow in their salvation. She continues to lead Bible studies in her community, at her home, and for her church. She writes daily devotions which can be found at exhalewithcookie.com.

www.ingramcontent.com/pod-product-compliance
Lightning Source LLC
Chambersburg PA
CBHW031355160726
47993CB00002B/993